Learn to Move!

I SWIM!

T0204908

By Bray Jacobson

Gareth Stevens
PUBLISHING

Please visit our website, www.garethstevens.com. For a free color catalog of all our high-quality books, call toll free 1-800-542-2595 or fax 1-877-542-2596.

Library of Congress Cataloging-in-Publication Data
Names: Jacobson, Bray, author.
Title: I swim! / Bray Jacobson.
Description: Buffalo, New York : Gareth Stevens Publishing, [2025] |
    Series: Learn to move! | Includes index.
Identifiers: LCCN 2023045843 | ISBN 9781482466102 (library binding) | ISBN
    9781482466096 (paperback) | ISBN 9781482466119 (ebook)
Subjects: LCSH: Swimming–Juvenile literature. | Aquatic sports–Juvenile
    literature.
Classification: LCC GV837.6 .J34 2025 | DDC 797.2/1–dc23/eng/20231023
LC record available at https://lccn.loc.gov/2023045843

First Edition

Published in 2025 by
Gareth Stevens Publishing
2544 Clinton Street
Buffalo, NY 14224

Editor: Kristen Nelson
Designer: Leslie Taylor

Photo credits: Cover Suzanne Tucker/Shutterstock.com; p. 5 Nataliya Turpitko/Shutterstock.com; pp. 7, 24 (towel) Ben Schonewille/Shutterstock.com; pp. 9, 24 (pool) Monkey Business Images/Shutterstock.com; pp. 11, 15 wavebreakmedia/Shutterstock.com; pp. 13, 23 seyomedo/Shutterstock.com; pp. 17, 24 (goggles) YanLev Alexey/Shutterstock.com; p. 19 Pongchart B/Shutterstock.com; p. 21 mariakray/Shutterstock.com.

Printed in the United States of America

CPSIA compliance information: Batch #CS25GS: For further information contact Gareth Stevens, New York, New York at 1-800-542-2595.

Find us on

Contents

It is time for my swim class!
I wear a bathing suit.

I bring my goggles.
I bring a towel.

It is warm at the pool!
I see my friend Greg.

Ms. Allie teaches my class. She tells us to get in the water.

We hold the side and kick.
I make a big splash!

We learn to move
our arms.
Ms. Allie helps Harper
try it.

It is time to float.
Noa goes first.
She floats on her back.

Drake puts his face in.
He blows bubbles!

It is Luna's turn.
She is scared.
She can do it!

We swim from one
wall to another.
I love to swim!

Words to Know

  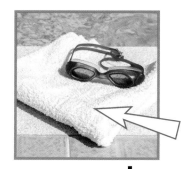

googles   pool   towel

Index